Chinese Hot Pot Cookbook

Many Tasty Chinese Hot Pot Recipes
that Could Easily Be Found in
Traditional Houses in China

Table of Contents

Introduction

Hotpots are simply awesome!

There is so little hassle involved because once the broth is prepared, your diners will be primarily doing their own cooking. Hot pot meals are so easy to put together, all you need to pull them off is some seafood, meat, vegetables, noodles or rice.

One of the best things about hotpot cooking is it is a great tool to use together friends and family together at the dinner table. Even children enjoy the fun of cooking their own food and fishing out of the tasty broth. It indeed is a fun way to cook and share a meal with friends and loved ones.

Many hot pot recipes include spices. If you are serving a hot pot to children, you might want to cut out a few of the spicier ingredients so it will be a tastier experience for the young ones at your dinner table.

Classic Wonton Hotpot

While wontons are technically considered a dumpling, to native Chinese people they are dumplings. For this particular recipe I highly recommend that you make the wontons as small as possible to prevent them from overcrowding your entire dish.

Serves: 4

Time: 40 Minutes

Ingredients:

- ½ Cup of Cabbage, Napa Style and Roughly Chopped
- 6 Ounces of Noodles, Egg Variety and Fresh
- 1 Carrot, Small in Size, Peeled and Cut Julienne Style
- 1 Cucumber, Small in Size, Peeled and Cut Julienne Style
- Some Chili Sauce

Wontons:

- ¼ Cup of Cabbage, Napa Variety and Chopped Coarsely
- 2 Ounces of Chicken, Skinless and Chopped into Small Pieces
- 6 Ounces of Pork, Butt Variety and Chopped into Small Pieces
- 4 Shrimp, Shelled, Deveined and Chopped Finely
- 2 Stalks of Onions, Green in Color and Minced
- 1 teaspoon of Oil, Sesame Variety and Dark in Color
- Dash of Salt and Pepper, For Taste

- Dash of Cornstarch

- 20 Skins of Wonton

Stock:

- 5 Cups of Chicken Stock, Homemade Preferable

- 1 tablespoon of Vegetables, Sichuan Variety, Drained and Finely Chopped

- ¼ teaspoons of Salt, For Taste

Directions:

1. The first thing you want to do is prepare your wontons. To do this combine your first 4 Ingredients for your wontons in a food processor and pulse until well blended.

2. Then add in your green onions and season with the next three ingredients. Mix together and set aside for later use.

3. Next take your corn starch and dust a smooth and flat surface with it. Place a teaspoon of your wonton mixture right into the middle of your wonton skin and dredge the edges with your egg. Fold again to form a triangle and seal the edges by pressing lightly together.

4. Fold your triangle and overlap it to the other side making sure that the corners stick well together. Seal again with a little pressure and your egg white and continue repeating the process until all of your ingredients have been used up. Cover your wontons with a damp cloth and set aside for later use.

5. Next prepare your stock. To do this is use a large sized pot and bring your first two ingredients together and bring the mixture to a boil. Once your mixture starts boiling reduce the heat and allow to cook for the next 5 minutes.

6. After the time remove from heat and transfer to a portable burner in the middle of your table. Next arrange you remaining ingredients around your broth on your table. To eat allow your guests to cook the ingredients in your broth to their liking.

Classic Pork and Rice Noodles

If you are looking for an authentic and truly classic Chinese recipe to enjoy, this is the perfect dish for you to prepare.

Serves: 4

Time: 15 Minutes

Ingredients:

- 5 Cups of Chicken Stock, Homemade Preferable
- 1 tablespoon of Shrimp, Dried
- 2 teaspoons of Salt, For Taste
- 3 tablespoons of Vinegar, Rice Variety
- 1 ½ tablespoons of Soy Sauce, Your Favorite Kind
- 6 Ounces of Cabbage, Napa Variety and Roughly Chopped

- 16 Ounces of Pork, Loin Variety and Thinly Sliced
- 6 Pieces of Mushrooms, Chinese Variety, Dried, Soaked and Finely Sliced
- 4 Ounces of Noodles, Thin and Soaked in Hot Water
- Some Oil, Sesame Variety
- 4 Stalks of Onions, Green in Color and Finely Chopped

Directions:

1. The first thing that you will want to do is prepare your stock. To do this use a large sized hot pot and combine your first five ingredients and place over high heat. Bring your mixture to a boil before reducing the heat to low. Over low heat let your mixture simmer for at least 5 minutes before removing from heat.

2. Strain your stock and transfer your strained mixture to your stockpot and transfer to a portable burn in the middle of your table.

3. Arrange your remaining ingredients around your stock. To eat allow your guests to cook the ingredients in your broth to their liking.

Classic Sukiyaki

This dish is considered to be one of the most popular hot pot dishes in China and once you get a taste of it yourself, you will not be surprised why. The flavor of this dish is the ultimate combination of sweetness and saltiness. I know you won't be able to get enough of it.

Serves: 4

Time: 20 Minutes

Ingredients:

- 1 tablespoon of Oil, Olive Variety
- 4 tablespoons of Sugar, White
- 2 tablespoons of Sake
- 4 tablespoons of Soy Sauce, Your Favorite Kind
- 8 Mushrooms, Small in Size and Chopped Finely
- 1 Pound of Beef, Sliced Thinly
- 1 Pack of Tofu, Firm and Cut into Small Cubes
- 1 Pack of Mushrooms, Enoki Variety
- 1 Onion, Sliced Thinly
- ½ Head of Cabbage, Napa Variety and Roughly Chopped

Directions:

1. The first thing that you will want to do is heat up a large sized pan over medium heat and add in your oil.

2. Once your oil is hot enough add in your beef and sear it on all sides.

3. Then add in your next 4 ingredients and toss thoroughly to coat.

4. Add in your tofu and remaining ingredients and stir to combine. Remove from heat.

5. Next transfer your hot pot to your table and allow your guests to cook the ingredients in your broth to their liking.

Meatball Packed Hot Pot

Out of any ingredient used in many Chinese style hot pot recipes, dumplings and meatballs tend to be the most popular. This is exactly what this dish incorporates and I know you are going to love it.

Serves: 4

Time: 25 Minutes

Ingredients:

- 6 Cups of Stock, Vegetable Variety and Homemade
- 3 Cloves of Garlic, Smashed and Peeled

- 1 Piece of Ginger, Peeled and Sliced Thinly
- 1 Cup of Mushrooms, Enoki Style, Washed and trimmed
- 1 Cabbage, Napa Style, Washed, Trimmed and Roughly Chopped
- 1 Cup of Shrimp, Peeled, Deveined and Washed
- 2 Blocks of Tofu, Dried, Fried and Finely Sliced
- 2 Carrots, Small in Size, Peeled and Sliced Thinly

Meatballs:

- 16 Oz. of Pork, Lean and Ground
- 2 Oz. of Fork Fat, Lean and Ground
- 2 Stalks of Onions, Green in Color and Finely Chopped
- 1 tablespoon of Ginger, Minced
- 1 Egg Yolk, Fresh
- 1 ½ tablespoons of Wine, Shaoxing Variety
- 1 tablespoon of Cornstarch
- 1 tablespoon of Oil, Sesame Variety
- 1 teaspoon of Soy Sauce, Your Favorite Kind
- 1 teaspoon of Salt, For Taste
- 1 teaspoon of Black Pepper, For Taste

Dipping Sauce:

- 2 tablespoons of Barbecue Sauce, Chinese Style
- 1 teaspoon of Oil, Sesame Variety
- 1 ½ tablespoons Soy Sauce, Your Favorite Kind
- 4 Stalks of Onions, Green in Color and Finely Chopped
- 1 teaspoon of Vinegar, Rice Variety
- ¼ Cup of Cilantro, Roughly Chopped

Directions:

1. The first thing you want to do is prepare your meatballs. To do this use a large sized bowl and mix together all of your Ingredients for your meatballs. Stir well to combine.

2. Then take a spoonful of your meat mixture and form it into even sized balls. Continue to do this until all of your meat mixture has been used up. Cover with a damp cloth and place into your fridge to chill.

3. Next prepare your dipping sauce. To do this use a small sized bowl and combine all of your dipping sauce ingredients together until thoroughly combined.

4. Then prepare your stock. To do this use a large size pot and combine your first 4 ingredients together and heat over high heat. Bring it to a boil and then remove from heat too cool. Once cool enough strain and make sure to discard the solids.

5. Transfer your strained stock into a large sized hot pot and transfer it to a portable burner in the middle of your table. Next arrange you remaining ingredients around your broth on your table. To eat allow your guests to cook the ingredients in your broth to their liking.

Spiced Lamb Hot Pot

With this delicious dish you will be using an ingredient known as Tobanjan, which will accompany your dish as a dipping sauce. It will help to give your dish a little extra kick while leaving you feeling completely full.

Serves: 2

Time: 25 Minutes

Ingredients:

- 24 Ounces of Lamb, Sliced Thinly
- ½ Cup of Cabbage, Napa Style and Roughly Chopped
- 4 Ounces of Mushrooms, Finely Sliced
- 4 Ounces of Mushrooms, Oyster Variety and Finely Sliced
- 3 Ounces of Bean Sprouts, Fresh, Washed and Trimmed
- 8 Cups of Stock, Beef Variety and Homemade Preferable

Dipping Sauce:

- 1 tablespoon of Tobanjan
- ¼ Cup of Wine, Rice Variety
- ¼ Cup of Soy Sauce, Your Favorite Kind
- 2 Cloves of Garlic, Peeled and Finely Grated
- 2 tablespoons of Sesame Seeds, Black in Color
- 1 tablespoon of Oil, Sesame Variety
- ¼ Cup of Vinegar, Rice Variety
- 1 tablespoon of Sugar, White
- 3 Stalks of Onions, Green in Color and Finely Chopped

Directions:

1. The first thing that you will want to do is prepare your dipping sauce. To do this combine all of your dipping sauce ingredients together into a food processor. Blend on the highest setting and blend for a couple of seconds until smooth in consistency.

2. Then use a large sized plate and arrange your first 4 ingredients in a neat pile.

3. Place your broth into your hot pot and place it over low heat to bring to a simmer using a portable burner.

4. Enjoy by letting your guests cook their food in the broth for as long as they wish.

Delicious Kimchi Jjigae

This delicious stew like dish is made with a bunch of ingredients that you can find all year round. Feel free to add whatever kind of ingredients you love to this dish to make it truly unique.

Serves: 3

Time: 40 Minutes

Ingredients:

- 4 Cups of Kimchi, Finely Chopped
- 1 tablespoon of Sugar, White

- 1 tablespoon of Pepper Flakes, For Taste
- 2 Onions, Green in Color and Finely Chopped
- 1 Onion, Large in Size, White in Color and Finely Chopped
- ½ Pack of Tofu, Firm and Cut into Small Pieces
- ½ Pound of Pork, Belly Variety
- Dash of Oil, Olive Variety
- Some Water, Warm

Directions:

1. First use a large sized hot pot and add in your water and kimchi.

2. Then add in your next 5 ingredients into it. Toss to combine.

3. Add in some additional water, making sure it is enough to submerge all of your ingredients.

4. Set over medium heat and allow your mixture to boil for the next 20 to 30 minutes.

5. After this time add in your tofu and allow to boil for an additional 5 minutes. Remove and serve right away.

The Ultimate Seafood Gumbo Hot Pot

If you are an avid seafood lover, then you need to try this recipe out for yourself! It is packed full of various types of seafood that you will absolutely drool over.

Serves: 6

Time: 1 Hour and 36 Minutes

Ingredients:

- 10 Cups of Stock, Chicken Variety and Homemade Preferable

- 1 tablespoon of Ginger, Minced

- 1 tablespoon of Garlic, Minced

- 6 Onions, Green in Color and Chopped Finely

- 4 Ounces of Noodles, Bean Thread Variety and Soaked

- 1 Pound of Cabbage, Napa Variety and Roughly Chopped

- 8 Scallops, Fresh and Sliced

- 4 Squid, Cut into Small Sized Rings

- 1 Pack of Tofu, Soft, Drained and Cut into Small Sized Cubes

- 12 Shrimp, Peeled, Deveined and Cut Butterfly Style

- 8 Oysters, Fully Shucked

- Some Soy Sauce, Your Favorite Kind

- Garlic Mustard Dipping Sauce:

- 3 tablespoons of Garlic, Minced

- 2 tablespoons of Sugar, White

- ¼ Cup of Water, Warm

- ¾ Cup of Mustard, Powdered Variety

- 2 tablespoons of Oil, Sesame Variety

- ¾ teaspoons of Oil, Vegetable Variety

- 2/3 Cup of Vinegar, Rice Wine Variety

Directions:

1. First combine your stock and wine in your hot pot and bring to a simmer over low heat.

2. Then arrange your remaining ingredients in separate bowls and plates on your table.

3. Remove your hot pot from heat and set into the center of your table. To eat allow your guests to cook the ingredients in your broth to their liking.

Classic Okayu

Another name for this dish is basic rice porridge. This is a great dish to make for those who have sensitive stomachs as it is not only delicious to eat, but it is also easy for the body to digest as well.

Serves: 1

Time: 30 Minutes

Ingredients:

- 3 Cups of Water, Warm
- Dash of Salt, For Taste

- ½ Cup of Rice, Uncooked

Directions:

1. The first thing that you will want to do is thoroughly wash your rice until the water begins to run clear.

2. Once thoroughly washed add your clean rice into a pot with your water and salt and stir to mix.

3. Cook over high heat while uncovered and cook for the next 20 minutes.

4. After this time serve right away and enjoy.

Easy Monkfish Hot Pot

While Monkfish itself may look as appetizing at first, but once you try this recipe for yourself, I know you will want to make it over and over again. It is a very tasty dish and will simply melt in your mouth. I know you will fall in love with it.

Serves: 4

Time: 10 Minutes

Ingredients:

- 16 Ounces of Monkfish, Cut into Thin Fillets
- 2 tablespoons of Wine, Shaoxing Variety
- 5 Cups of Stock, Chicken Variety and Homemade Preferable
- 2 Ounces of Noodles, Vermicelli Variety, Soaked and Drained
- ½ Cup of Cabbage, Napa Variety and Roughly Chopped
- 2 Blocks of Tofu, Firm and Cut into Quarters
- 3 Ounces of Mushrooms, Straw Variety and Thinly Sliced
- 3 Ounces of Mushrooms, Oyster Variety, Trimmed and Finely Sliced
- 2 Stalks of Onions, Green in Color and Finely Sliced
- 2 tablespoons of Suan Cai

Directions:

1. First combine your stock and wine in your hot pot and bring to a simmer over low heat.

2. Then arrange your remaining ingredients in separate bowls and plates on your table.

3. Remove your hot pot from heat and set into the center of your table. To eat allow your guests to cook the ingredients in your broth to their liking.

Easy Shabu

This is perhaps one of the most famous hot pot dishes that you will find in native China today. This dish is mostly made up of raw veggies and thin strips of meat, making it not only incredibly delicious, but relatively easy to make as well.

Serves: 4

Time: 30 Minutes

Ingredients:

- 4 Mushrooms, Shiitake Variety and Finely Chopped

- 12 to 15 Ounces of Steak, Sliced Thinly
- 2 Cups of Cabbage, Napa Variety and Roughly Chopped
- 2 Cups of Spinach, Baby Variety and Roughly Chopped
- 2 Leeks, Cut into Small Pieces
- 12 Ounces of Tofu, Firm and Cut into Small Pieces

Directions:

1. The first thing that you will want to do is place your strips of meat onto a plate and set to chill in your fridge.

2. Next arrange your veggies onto another plate and set into your fridge to chill.

3. Use a large sized pot and add in at least 8 cups of water. Set over high heat and bring the water to a boil.

4. Using a grilling sheet, place your meats and veggies on top of the boiling water and cook until done to your desired likeness.

5. Remove and serve right away. Enjoy!

Filling Vegetable and Pork Hot Pot

If you are looking for a filling hot pot dish to make, this is the perfect dish for you. Not only is it incredibly filling, but the ginger you will use help to make this dish one that even the pickiest eaters will fall in love with.

Serves: 4

Time: 30 Minutes

Ingredients:

- 16 Ounces of Pork, Shoulder Only and Sliced Thinly
- 1 Carrot, Fresh, Peeled and Sliced Thinly
- 1 Cup of Turnips, Fresh, Peeled and Thinly Sliced
- 1 Cup of Bean Sprouts, Washed and Trimmed
- 6 Stalks of Onions, Green in Color and Roughly Chopped
- 6 Cups of Stock, Pork Variety and Homemade Preferable
- 4 tablespoons of Soy Sauce, Your Favorite Kind
- 3 tablespoons of Wine, Shaoxing Variety
- 3 teaspoons of Brown Sugar, Light and Packed
- 1 Piece of Ginger, Peeled and Finely Sliced
- 1 tablespoon of Vinegar, Balsamic Variety
- 3 teaspoons of Chili Garlic Sauce, Chinese Variety
- 3 Cloves of Garlic, Finely Chopped
- 1 teaspoon of Cinnamon, Ground
- 4 teaspoons of Cornstarch
- 2 tablespoons of Water, Cold
- 3 tablespoons of Sesame Seeds, Toasted and Black in Color

Directions:

1. First prepare your stock. To do this add in your pork stock, favorite kind of soy sauce, wine, light brown sugar, ginger, vinegar, chili garlic sauce, chopped garlic and cinnamon to a hot pot. Bring this mixture to a boil over high heat and then reduce the heat. Simmer for the next 2 ½ hours.

2. After this time remove from heat and drain the solids from the broth. Return back to your hot pot. Place over low heat.

3. Dissolve your cornstarch with your water and add into your broth. Stir constantly until your broth is thick in consistency. This should take about 2 minutes. After this time transfer your hot pot to your portable burner and place it into the middle of your table.

4. Arrange your remaining ingredients on serving plates on your table. To eat allow your guests to cook the ingredients in your broth to their liking.

Traditional Nabeyaki Udon

While the name itself may seem like a mouthful, I know you are going to love this recipe. This is a classic noodle hot pot stuffed full of healthy veggies that make for a great tasting meal.

Serves: 2

Time: 1 Hour

Ingredients:

- 3 tablespoons of Mirin
- 1 tablespoon of Salt, For Taste
- 1 tablespoon of Ginger, Grated Finely
- 3 Cloves of Garlic, Minced
- 1/3 Cup of Soy Sauce, Your Favorite Kind
- 5 Eggs, Large in Size and Beaten
- 20 Ounces of Noodles, Udon Variety
- 1 Pound of Chicken Thighs, Boneless and Skinless Variety
- 2 Leeks, Sliced Finely
- 2 Carrots, Peeled and Sliced Thinly
- 6 Ounces of Spinach Leave, Fresh and Roughly Torn
- 48 Ounces of Dashi

Directions:

1. First bring a large sized pot of water to a boil over high heat. Add in your spinach and cook for no more than a minute. Remove and drain. Set aside.

2. Next mix together your 5 ingredients together in a large sized hot pot and set over medium heat.

3. Once piping hot add in your carrots and thinly sliced leeks. Stir thoroughly to combine.

4. Last add in your chicken and drizzle in your beaten eggs.

5. Remove from heat and set into the middle of your table on a portable burner.

6. Next arrange you remaining ingredients around your broth on your table. To eat allow your guests to cook the ingredients in your broth to their liking.

Simple Halibut Hot Pot

If you are a huge fan of Halibut, you won't be able to resist the taste of this dish. It is easy to make and one of the simplest hot pot recipes you will ever put together.

Serves: 4

Time: 15 Minutes

Ingredients:

- 24 Ounces of Halibut, Cut into Thin Fillets
- ½ teaspoons of Salt, For Taste
- 5 Cups of Stock, Vegetable Variety and Homemade Preferable

- ¼ tablespoons of Oyster Sauce
- ½ tablespoons of Wine, Shaoxing Variety
- 3 Ounces of Noodles, Vermicelli Variety, Soaked and Drained
- ½ Cup of Cabbage, Napa Variety and Roughly Chopped
- 3 Stalks of Onions, Green in Color and Roughly Chopped
- 1 Block of Tofu, Firm and Trimmed
- 6 Ounces of Mushrooms, Oyster Variety and Trimmed
- 3 Ounces of Bean Sprouts, Washed and Trimmed
- 2 tablespoons of Oil, Chili Variety

Directions:

1. The first thing you want to do is lightly season both sides of your fish with some salt. Cover and place in your fridge to chill for the next 30 minutes.

2. After this time remove your fish with a paper towel lightly. Set aside for later use.

3. Best prepare your stock. To do this use a large-sized hot pot and combine your next 4 ingredients together. Bring to a

boil over high heat before reducing to a simmer over low heat. After five minutes remove from heat.

4. Transfer your stock to a portable burner on your table and arrange your remaining ingredients around it. To eat allow your guests to cook the ingredients in your broth to their liking.

Easy Red Snapper Hot Pot

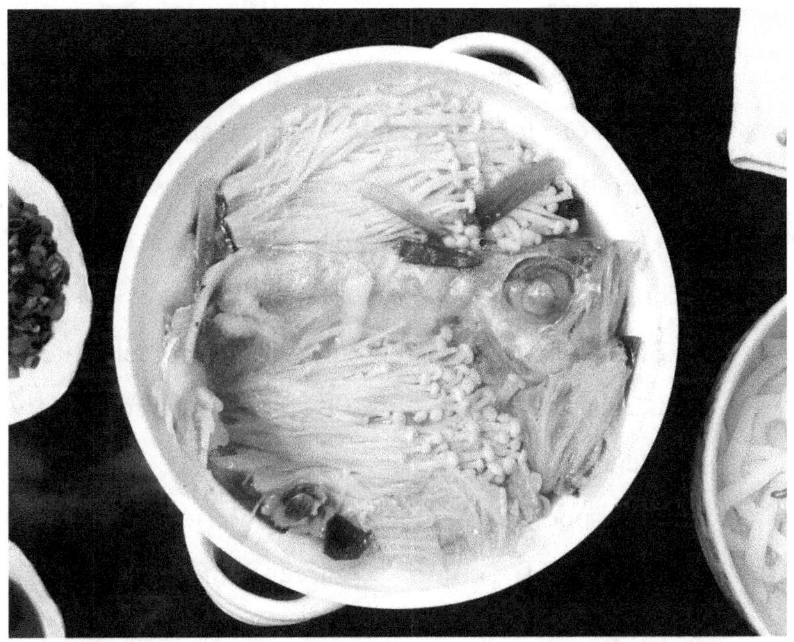

Here is yet another great tasting seafood inspired hot pot that I know you won't be able to help but enjoy. With this particular recipe you will be using the entire fish so don't worry if you have too much on your hands. No part of it will go to waste.

Serves: 4

Time: 40 Minutes

Ingredients:

- 1 Red Snapper, Whole, Cleaned and Scaled
- Dash of Salt, For Curing
- 5 Cups of Stock, Vegetable Variety and Homemade Preferable
- ½ Cup of Cabbage, Napa Variety and Roughly Chopped
- 3 Stalks of Onions, Green in Color and Finely Sliced
- 6 Ounces of Mushrooms, Oyster Variety and Finely Sliced
- 2 tablespoons of Wine, Shaoxing Variety
- 1 Ounce of Tom Yao, Green Only and Finely Chopped
- 2 tablespoons of Suan Cai

Directions:

1. Once your snapper has been cleaned and scaled, lightly cure it with a light sprinkling of salt on both sides of it and leave out for the next 30 minutes.

2. After this time wipe your red snapper with a paper towel to dry.

3. Place your stock into a hot pot in the middle of your table on a portable burner and allow it to come to a simmer.

4. Next arrange you remaining ingredients around your broth on your table. To eat allow your guests to cook the ingredients in your broth to their liking.

Chinese Style Creamy Hot Pot

This is a Chinese style hot pot recipe that I know you are going to fall in love with. The potatoes and creamy stock that make up the bulk of this recipe make this a dish that you won't soon forget.

Serves: 4

Time: 30 Minutes

Ingredients:

- 18 Ounces of Pork, Belly and Thinly Sliced
- 8 Ounces of Chicken, Uncooked and Thinly Sliced
- 8 Ounces of Shrimp, Shelled and Deveined
- 8 Ounces of Fish Balls, Chinese Style
- 1 Block of Tofu, Firm and Cut into Quarters
- 1 Cup of Bean Sprouts, Fresh, Washed and Trimmed
- 1 Cup of Mushrooms, Straw Variety, Washed and Finely Sliced
- ¼ Cup of Tong Ho, Washed and Trimmed

Stock:

- 3 Cups of Stock, Chicken Variety and Homemade Preferable
- 3 Cups of Stock, Vegetable Variety and Homemade Preferable
- 1 Potato, Small in Size, Peeled and Finely Sliced
- 1 Piece of Ginger, Peeled and Thinly Sliced
- 3 Stalks of Onions, Green in Color and Finely Chopped
- 1 Pieces of Mushroom, Chinese Variety, Dried and Soaked
- 2 tablespoons of Wine, Shaozing Variety

- Dash of Salt and Pepper, For Taste

Directions:

1. The first thing that you will want to do is prepare your stock. To do this combine both your chicken and vegetable stock together in a large sized hot pot. Bring this mixture to a boil over high heat and then reduce the heat to low. Allow to simmer for at least a couple of minutes.

2. Then add in your potato and cook for an additional 5 minutes.

3. After this time add in your remaining stock ingredients. Allow your mixture to simmer for at least 45 minutes.

4. After this time remove from heat and transfer to a portable burner in the middle of your table.

5. Arrange your ingredients onto serving dishes around your hot pot. To eat allow your guests to cook the ingredients in your broth to their liking.

Easy Sweet and Sour Hot Pot

If you are a huge fan of classic sweet and sour chicken from your favorite Chinese restaurant, then you need to give this recipe a try. This is a dish that I recommend serving during the cold winter season as it will warm you right up!

Serves: 4

Time: 20 Minutes

Ingredients:

- 5 Cups of Stock, Chicken Variety
- 2 tablespoons of Soy Sauce, Light and Your Favorite Kind
- 2 tablespoons of Vinegar
- 2 teaspoons of Oil, Sesame Variety
- 1 teaspoon of Peppercorn, Sichuan Variety
- 2 tablespoons of Cornstarch
- 4 tablespoons of Water, Cold
- 12 Ounces of Chicken Fillets, Finely Sliced
- 4 Slices of Ham, Chinese Style and Finely Sliced
- 2 teaspoons of Salt, For Taste
- 1 teaspoon of Sugar, White
- 1 Block of Tofu, Firm and Finely Diced
- ½ Cup of Bamboo Shoots, Sliced Thinly
- 1 Carrot, Peeled and Sliced Thinly
- 4 Pieces of Mushrooms, Chinese Style and Soaked
- ½ Cup of Mushrooms, Woodear Variety and Sliced Finely
- 4 Eggs, Small in Size and Beaten
- ¼ Cup of Coriander Leaves, Roughly Chopped
- 1 Piece of Ginger, Peeled and Finely Grated
- 6 Stalks of Onions, Green in Color and Finely Chopped

Directions:

1. First prepare your stock. To do this combine your first 6 ingredients in a large sized hot pot and heat over high heat.

2. Bring to a boil before reducing the heat to low. Slowly add in your cornstarch dissolved in your cold water and stir until thick in consistency.

3. Remove from heat and place onto a portable burner in the center of your table.

4. Next arrange you remaining ingredients around your broth on your table. To eat allow your guests to cook the ingredients in your broth to their liking.

Clam Packed Hot Pot

If there is one ingredient that is perfect for hot pot recipes, it is clams. Clams help to make a hot pot dish flavorful and incredibly delicious to eat.

Serves: 4

Time: 10 Minutes

Ingredients:

- 48 Clams, Cleaned and Shells Discarded
- 2 Blocks of Tofu, Fried and Thinly Sliced
- 3 Stalks of Onions, Green in Color and Finely Sliced

- 7 Ounces of Mushrooms, Oyster Variety and Finely Sliced
- ¼ Cup of Tom Yao Leaves, Fresh and Finely Sliced
- 5 Cups of Stock, Chicken Variety and Homemade Preferable
- Dash of Pepper, Szechuan Variety
- Some Suan Cai

Directions:

1. Arrange all of your ingredients in separate bowls and plates on your table.

2. Place your hot pot into the center of your table.

3. To eat allow your guests to cook the ingredients in your broth to their liking.

Mongolian Style Lamb Hot Pot

This is a traditional, yet delicious hot pot recipe that you won't be able to get enough of. It is another dish that is made with lamb and that will leave you feeling completely satisfied.

Serves: 6

Time: 10 Minutes

Ingredients:

- 24 Ounces of Lamb, Sliced Thinly

- 8 Ounces of Noodles, Cellophane Variety and Soaked Completely
- 9 Ounces of Cabbage, Chinese Variety, Washed and Trimmed
- 1 Carrot, Peeled and Sliced Thinly
- 8 Stalks of Onions, Green in Color and White and Green Parts Separated
- 12 Cups of Stock, Beef or Vegetable Variety

Dipping Sauce:

- 5 tablespoons of Paste, Sesame Variety
- 5 tablespoons of Bean Paste, Fermented
- 6 tablespoons of Wine, Shaoxing Variety
- 6 tablespoons of Soy Sauce, Your Favorite Kind
- 4 tablespoons of Oil, Chili Variety
- 4 tablespoons of Oil, Sesame Variety
- A Few Drops of Water

Directions:

1. First prepare your dipping sauce. To do this combine all of your dipping sauce ingredients together in a small sized bowl, making sure to stir to thoroughly combine. Set aside.

2. Next arrange you remaining ingredients around your broth on your table. To eat allow your guests to cook the ingredients in your broth to their liking.

Traditional Duck Hot Pot

This is as traditional a Chinese hot pot dish that you are ever going to find. This is an easy adaptation to traditional soups from Hong Kong and is most popular for its soothing taste that you won't be able to resist.

Serves: 4

Time: 35 Minutes

Ingredients:

- 24 Ounces of Duck, Wild and Bones Only
- 24 Ounces of Chicken, Bones Only

- 8 Cups of Stock, Chicken Variety and Homemade Preferable
- 1/3 Cup of Wine, Rice Variety
- 2 Stalks of Onions, Green in Color and Finely Sliced
- 1 Piece of Ginger, Peeled and Smashed
- Dash of Salt and Pepper, For Taste
- 16 Ounces of Duck, Wild Variety and Thinly Sliced
- ½ Cup of Bamboo Shoots, Finely Sliced
- 12 Ounces of Bok Choy, Baby Variety and Finely Sliced
- 4 Ounces of Ham, Chinese Style and Finely Sliced

Dipping Sauce:

- ½ Cup of Vinegar, Black in Color and Chinese Style
- 3 tablespoons of Soy Sauce, Your Favorite Kind

Directions:

1. Use a large sized hot pot and combine your homemade chicken stock and wild duck together. Bring this mixture to a boil over high heat before reducing the heat to low. Allow your mixture to simmer.

2. Then add in your rice wine, chopped green onions and ginger. Bring this mixture to a boil before reducing the heat

to low again. Allow your mixture to simmer for at least one hour.

3. Season your dish with another dash of salt and pepper and continue simmering for another 5 minutes. Remove from heat and strain. Transfer your mixture back into your hot pot.

4. Next prepare your dipping sauce. To do this combine your dipping sauce ingredients together, making sure to mix well until thoroughly combined.

5. Next arrange you remaining ingredients around your broth on your table. To eat allow your guests to cook the ingredients in your broth to their liking.

Simple Noodle Hot Pot

This is an easy and simple dish that you can make as a tasty snack or even as a light and hearty meal. A word of caution: this is a spicy dish so take care on the amount of spice you add into it.

Serves: 4

Time: 25 Minutes

Ingredients:

- 6 Cups of Stock, Chicken Variety and Homemade Preferable
- 12 Ounces of Noodle, Wheat Variety, Soaked and Drained

- 2 teaspoons of Oil, Sesame Variety and Dark in Color
- 1 tablespoon of Sesame, Paste Only
- 2 tablespoons of Chili Paste
- 1 tablespoon of Vinegar, Rice Wine Variety
- 2 teaspoons of Peppercorns, Sichuan Variety
- ½ Cup of Bean Sprouts, Fresh
- 2 Onions, Small in Size, White in Color, Peeled and Finely Chopped
- ¼ Cup of Coriander Leaves, Fresh
- 4 Ounces of Vegetables, Chinese Style and Preserved

Beef Topping:

- 2 Cloves of Garlic, Minced
- 12 Ounces of Beef, Finely Sliced
- ½ a Piece of Ginger, Peeled and Grated
- 2 Pieces of Red Chili, Seeded and Finely Chopped
- 1 tablespoon of Soy Sauce, Your Favorite Kind
- 2 tablespoons of Wine, Shaoxing Variety

Directions:

1. The first thing that you will want to do is prepare your meat topping. To do this use a large sized bowl and combine all of your Ingredients for your beef topping together and leave to marinate for at least an hour.

2. Next prepare your stock. To do this use a large sized hot pot and combine your first 3 ingredients together and bring to a simmer over low heat.

3. Next heat up your peppercorns in a small sized pan placed over medium heat. Roast your peppercorns until they turn fragrant. Then remove from heat. Pour into a mortar and pestle, making sure to crush them lightly.

4. Add your crushed peppercorns into your broth and simmer for at least one minute. Remove from heat and transfer to a portable burner.

5. Next arrange you remaining ingredients around your broth on your table. To eat allow your guests to cook the ingredients in your broth to their liking.

Crab Packed Hot Pot

Crabs are considered to be a delicacy in different parts of China. Not only will this dish help fill you up, but it will also help you to reap various medical benefits as well.

Serves: 4

Time: 15 Minutes

Ingredients:

- 32 Ounces of Crab, Fresh
- 4 Cups of Stock, Vegetable Variety and Homemade Preferable

- 4 tablespoons of Soy Sauce, Your Favorite Kind

- 2 tablespoons of Wine, Rice Variety

- 1 Ounce of Noodles, Vermicelli Variety, Soaked and Drained

- ½ Cup of Cabbage, Napa Variety, Roughly Chopped

- 1 Block of Tofu, Firm and Finely Diced

- 2 Stalks of Onions, Green in Color and Finely Sliced

- 4 Ounces of Mushrooms, Oyster Variety and Finely Sliced

Directions:

1. The first thing that you will want to do is prepare your crab. To do this use a knife and slice off the strips of the shell and cut into the claws.

2. Then prepare your broth by mixing together your next 3 ingredients in your hot pot. Heat over high heat to bring it to a boil before reducing the heat to a simmer. Allow to simmer for at least 5 minutes. Remove from heat.

3. Transfer your hot pot to a portable burn in the middle of your table.

4. Then arrange your remaining ingredients around your stock. To eat allow your guests to cook the ingredients in your broth to their liking.

Cantonese Style Hot Pot

This is a seafood inspired hot pot that even the pickiest eaters won't be able to turn down. Packed full of delicious seafood I know you are going to want to make this dish over and over again.

Serves: 4

Time: 10 Minutes

Ingredients:

- 8 Ounces of Sea Bass, Fresh and Cut into Fillets
- 12 Ounces of Prawns, Large in Size, Fresh, Shelled and Cut into Halves
- 8 Pieces of Scallops, Large in Size
- 12 Ounces of Celery, Fresh and Finely Sliced
- 12 Ounces of Cabbage, Napa Variety, Washed and Trimmed
- ¼ Cup of Watercress, Washed and Trimmed
- 2 Blocks of Tofu, Firm and Cut into Quarters
- 12 Ounces of Noodles, Egg Variety and Drained
- 8 Cups of Stock, Vegetable Variety and Homemade Preferable

Dipping Sauce:

- 4 Eggs, Large in Size
- Some Soy Sauce, Your Favorite Kind
- Some Oil, Sesame Variety
- Some Chili Sauce, Chinese Style

Directions:

1. Use a large sized plate and arrange your first 8 ingredients nicely into it.

2. Then place your next three ingredients into smaller individual dishes.

3. Next arrange you remaining ingredients around your broth on your table. To eat allow your guests to cook the ingredients in your broth to their liking.

Yunnan Style Chicken

The whole purpose of the Yunnan cuisine is to focus more on the natural taste of all of the ingredients used rather than focus on fake tastes. One of the ingredients that you will use more predominantly in this dish is Ginger and it really compliments the taste of chicken in this dish.

Serves: 4

Time: 17 Minutes

Ingredients:

- 5 Cups of Stock, Chicken Variety
- 1 teaspoon of Wine, Rice Variety
- 1 Piece of Ginger, Peeled and Finely Sliced
- ½ teaspoons of Salt, For Taste
- 16 Ounces of Chicken Breast, Thinly Sliced
- 3 Ounces of Ham, Chinese Style and Thinly Sliced
- ½ Cup of Bok Choy, Baby Variety and Roughly Chopped
- Dash of Oil, Chili Variety

Directions:

1. The first thing you want to do is to prepare your stock. To do this use a large-sized hot pot and combine your first 4 ingredients together.

2. Heat over high heat and bring this mixture to a boil before reducing the heat to low.

3. Cook for at least 15 minutes and then remove from heat.

4. Strain your stock and transfer back to your hot pot.

5. Next arrange you remaining ingredients around your broth on your table.

6. To eat allow your guests to cook the ingredients in your broth to their liking.

Classic Duck Dumpling Stuffed Hot Pot

It is no secret that native Chinese people love their dumplings and once you get a taste of this recipe you won't be able to get enough of them either!

Serves: 4

Time: 30 Minutes

Ingredients:

- 16 Ounces of Duck Breasts, Sliced Thinly
- ¼ Cup of Flour, Buckwheat Variety
- 4 Cups of Stock, Vegetable Variety and Homemade Preferable
- ½ Cup of Wine, Rice Variety
- ¾ Cup of Soy Sauce, Light and Your Favorite Kind
- 3 Stalks of Onions, Green in Color and Finely Sliced
- ½ Cup of Cabbage, Napa Variety and Roughly Chopped
- 4 Ounces of Noodles, Fresh and Egg Variety
- ½ Cup of Spinach, Roughly Torn
- 4 teaspoons of Oil, Sesame Variety

Dumplings:

- 12 Ounces of Duck Breast, Skinless, Boneless and Chopped into Small Pieces
- 2 tablespoons of Flour, Buckwheat Variety
- ¼ Cup of Onions, Green in Color and Sliced Thinly
- ½ teaspoons of Pepper, Ground and For Taste
- 1 teaspoon of Wine, Rice Variety
- 1 Egg, Large in Size and Beaten

Directions:

1. First prepare your dumplings. To do this combine all of your Ingredients for the dumplings into a food processor and pulse until it is coarse in consistency. Transfer to a bowl and cover with a damp cloth. Set aside for later use.

2. Then take your duck breast and roll them in your flour one piece at a time. Set aside for later use.

3. Next prepare your broth. To do this combine your first 3 ingredients together and place over high heat. Once your mixture is boiling reduce the heat to low and add in your dumplings one tablespoon at a time. Continue to simmer your mixture for the next 3 minutes.

4. Then add in your next for ingredients and cover. Allowed to simmer for the next 5 minutes.

5. After this time on cover and adding your floured duck slices. Continue to simmer for the next 3 minutes or until your duck is cooked to perfection. Remove from heat and serve with your oil. Enjoy.

Cantonese Surf and Turf

Here is a traditional Chinese hot pot sea food recipe that every seafood lover won't be able to resist. Feel free to add any additional ingredients that you like to make this dish truly your own creation.

Serves: 4

Time: 10 Minutes

Ingredients:

- 12 Ounces of Prawns, Shelled and Cut into Halves
- 8 Ounces of Sea Bass, Cut into Fillets
- 8 Pieces of Scallops, Large in Size
- 8 Ounces of Steak, Skirt Variety and Thinly Sliced
- 12 Ounces of Celery, Chinese Style and Thinly Sliced
- ½ Cup of Cabbage, Napa Style and Roughly Chopped
- ¼ Cup of Watercress, Washed and Trimmed
- 2 Blocks of Tofu, Cut into Quarters
- 8 Ounces of Noodles, Egg Variety and Drained
- 8 Cups of Stock, Beef Variety

Dipping Sauce:

- 6 Eggs, Large in Size and Beaten
- Some Soy Sauce, Your Favorite Kind
- Some Oil, Sesame Variety
- Some Chili Paste

Directions:

1. First arrange all of your ingredients except for your stock into small individual dishes.

2. Next place for broth in a large sized hot pot in the middle of your table.

3. Next arrange your dishes around your broth on your table. To eat allow your guests to cook the ingredients in your broth to their liking.

Pork Ribs Hot Pot

A hot pot can be used to prepare way more than just soups. The ingredients in this Pork Ribs dish contributes nicely to the full-bodied taste that makes it such a popular and favorite hot pot dish.

Serves: 4-6

Time: 20 minutes

Ingredients:

- 1 teaspoon ketchup
- 4 or 5 ginger slices
- 1 ½ lbs. pork rib meat, sliced very thinly

- 5 tablespoons of vinegar

- 2 ½ tablespoons of sugar, granulated

- 1 teaspoon soy sauce, light

- ½ cup water, filtered

- dipping sauces of your choice

Directions:

1. Heat a large pot, add oil then sauté the ginger slices. Add the water and seasoning.

2. Bring the ingredients to a boil. Allow to thicken and stir in the ketchup.

3. Pour broth into the hotpot on the table. Diners can use chopsticks to dip pork slices into the hot broth.

4. Set out dipping sauces of your choice also.

Chinese Mung Bean Hot Pot

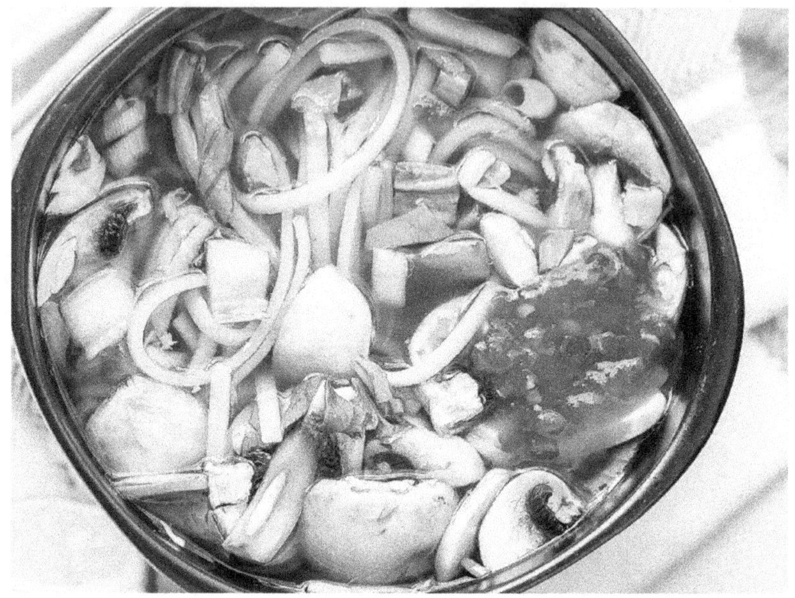

This is a yummy Chinese hot pot dish that is filled with chicken, noodles, and vegetables. It is a healthy and comforting dish.

Serves: 6

Time: 35 minutes

Ingredients:

- ½ cup rice vinegar
- 1/3 cup soy sauce, low-sodium

- 1 ½ tablespoon of sesame oil

- 5 slices ginger, fresh

- 6 cups chicken stock, low-sodium

- 6 cups filtered water

- 5 cloves garlic, cracked

- 1 lb. Chicken thighs, boneless, thinly sliced

- 5-ounces rice noodles

- 1 bunch scallions

- 1 ½ cups mung bean sprouts

- 8-ounces mushrooms

- 4 cups Bok choy, baby leaves, chopped

Directions:

1. Bring the water, ginger, garlic, vinegar, soy sauce, sesame oil and chicken stock to a boil in a large pot.

2. Toss in your noodles then stir before switching off the heat.

3. Chop the veggies and place them in serving bowls.

4. Fill your serving bowls with vegetables and some chili sauce.

5. Ladle the boiling soup over veggies, allowing them to cook for five minutes or so.

Vegan Chinese Hot Pot

This is a very hearty hot pot dish, filled with veggies and tofu that makes for a filling vegan meal.

Serves: 2-4

Time: 8 hours 35 minutes (including 8 hours slow cooker time)

Ingredients:

For soup:

- 3 tablespoon soy sauce, low-sodium

- 60 ounces vegetable stock

- 2 celery sticks, sliced

- 1×8-ounce can bamboo shoots, drained

- 2 teaspoons garlic paste

- 1×8-ounce can water chestnuts, sliced, drained

- 1 onion, medium, chopped

- 1 cup carrots, sliced

- 2 teaspoons ginger, paste

- 2 teaspoons fish sauce

- ½ teaspoon pepper flakes, red

Additions:

- bottled ginger sauce

- baby Bok choy, 2 bunches, sliced

- 8-ounces tofu, firm, drained, cubed

- button mushrooms, 4-ounces, sliced

- 1-ounce snow peas, cut with strings removed

- 6 green onions, chopped

Directions:

1. Add your soup ingredients into your hot pot then set to cook on low for 8 hours.

2. Add in your additions excluding a bit of your green onions, about 20 minutes before serving. Save the extra green onions for garnish.

3. Cook for 20 minutes, then transfer to the hot pot on the serving table.

4. Serve the spoonful of ginger soy sauce with every soup bowl. Garnish them with the reserved green onions. Allow your diners to fill their bowls from the hot pot.

Mushroom Ginger Hot Pot

In this dish the combination of mushrooms and ginger go so well together, it makes a great meal especially on a chilly day!

Serves: 2-4

Time: 1 hour 5 minutes

Ingredients:

- 2 tablespoons soy sauce
- 1 tomato, chopped

- 1×15-ounce can of coconut milk, light
- rice noodles, cooked to serve
- black pepper to taste
- ½ lime, juice only
- 1 red bell pepper, sliced
- pinch of sea salt, coarse
- 1 tablespoon sesame oil
- 1 red onion, sliced
- 4 cups vegetable broth
- 1 tablespoon cornstarch
- 3 cloves garlic, minced
- 2 tablespoons lemongrass, minced
- ½ teaspoon pepper flakes, red, crushed
- ¼ teaspoon cinnamon, ground
- 1 tablespoon ginger, minced
- Shiitake mushrooms, 1-ounce, dried
- 2 x star anise
- Dipping sauces (your preferred)

Directions:

1. Heat broth and cornstarch in a pot over medium heat. Set aside

2. Sauté pepper and onion in oil with some salt, until the onions soften.

3. Add ginger, lemongrass, garlic, and pepper flakes. Combine well. Cook until the mixture until it becomes fragrant. Add the broth and cornstarch mixture.

4. Add tomatoes, soy sauce, mushrooms, pepper, cinnamon, and star anise. Now, stir the mixture for about 10 minutes or until it thickens. Cover the hot pot. Bring to a boil.

5. Once it has reached a boil put in on medium low heat. Cover and cook for about 30 minutes or until the mushrooms soften completely. Add the coconut milk and lime.

6. Transfer hot pot to heated base on the serving table.

7. Serve your diners pieces of chicken, tofu or beef with chopsticks, and dipping sauce.

Pork Curry Hot Pot

This dish offers a bold flavor like red curry; it is also a versatile enough dish to serve on nights you are entertaining.

Serves: 4

Time: 40 minutes

Ingredients:

For broth:

- 1lb cooked rice noodles

- 1-inch slice fresh ginger

- 8 cups vegetable stock, low-sodium

- 1 tablespoon olive oil

- 5 garlic cloves, minced

- 3×15-ounce cans coconut milk

- 4-6 tablespoons curry paste, red

Protein:

- 2lb. Pork, thinly sliced

- 2 cups sweet potatoes, peeled and cubed

- 2 cups squash, cut and cubed

- 1 ½ cups peas

- 2 onions, chopped

- 3 cups mushrooms, sliced

- 1 cup cauliflower, chopped

- 2 cups broccoli, chopped

- 2 red bell peppers, diced

Directions:

1. Use a large stockpot to heat your oil over medium high heat. Add your garlic and ginger.

2. Sauté for a couple of minutes and stir until the garlic becomes fragrant. Add coconut milk and vegetable stock and stir to combine.

3. Set heat to simmer and continue to cook for about 10 minutes. Add three or four tablespoons of curry paste.

4. Whisk until it dissolves, add more curry paste to taste.

5. Cover pot, and simmer for five minutes. Remove the ginger.

6. Pour the broth into the hotpot and place it on the burn on the serving table. Ladle broth into individual bowls.

7. Allow your diners to cook meat in broth and place in their own bowls.

8. Have dipping sauce and garnish ingredients on the serving table.

Conclusion

These recipes have genuinely given me so much enjoyment making them that I was compelled to share. I hope that you were able to gain just as much enjoyment out of all 30 Chinese Hotpot recipes from your own kitchen. All the recipes featured were strategically select so as to allow you to be able to find the ingredients in your local stores easily. So, there shouldn't be any accessibility issues holding you back.

With that in mind, go ahead and grab your favorite recipe and get your cooking on! Thank you again for opting to spend your time with me in this Chinese Hotpot Recipes Cookbook. Have yourselves an amazing day!

Bye!

www.ingramcontent.com/pod-product-compliance
Lightning Source LLC
Chambersburg PA
CBHW071546150726
48000CB00002B/962